CALLED TO LEAD

An Anthology of Prolific Leadership

Volume 1

By
Dr. Monique Rodgers & An Iconic Co-Author Team Of Leaders Making A Difference In The World Through Leadership

ISBN:9798831872392

Published by Shooting Stars Publishing House

Printed in the United States of America

DEDICATION

This book is dedicated to leaders in ministry, the marketplace, church, business, music, entertainment industry, law, small business leaders, film, nursing, entrepreneurs, and all leaders who have understood the mandated call of leadership that is needed for such a time as this.

CONTENTS

ABOUT THE LEADER

Dr. Evangelist Tamike Brown

Dr. Evangelist Tamike Brown is an Anointed Woman of God. She's An Author, Co-Author, Founder and President of Outreach International Foundation Ministry, Tamike Brown Ministries, God

Anointed Fire Vessels Television Network, TKKJ Video & Audio Production Company, Discover You With Tamike, LLC, **Salvation With Fire®** Television and Radio Show, Atlanta Georgia.

Her Evangelistic Ministry is determined to see people **"Saved"** from all parts of the world through the power of God's Holy Word. Reaching people National and International through street ministry, prayer station, outreach events, speaking engagements, women conferences, crusades, virtual events, etc.

Tamike was born and raised in Cordele, Georgia by her grandmother the late Mrs. Maggie Wilkins Odom 'aka" her mother. She currently resides in Atlanta, GA and is the mother of three lovely children and one sister. Kerwin, Kierra, Josh, and Dorothy.

She currently attends Temple of Prayer Worship Center in Fairburn, GA under the leadership of Bishop Aaron B. Lackey Sr., and First Lady Lakita Lackey.

Evangelist Brown received the call of God for her life in 2000 to evangelize the world with her Holy Boldness and her God given message **"Salvation With Fire".** She is determined to fulfill her God given **"Destiny"** in "Changing Nations for the Glory of God."

- In 2004 she received her ministerial licensed from The Sure Foundation Theological Fellowship Institute in Seminole, Florida.
- In 2009 she was a Salutatorian Graduate from The School of Ministry at Covenant Church of Jesus Christ in Macon, GA.
- In 2010 she received her bachelor's degree from DeVry University in Atlanta, GA. with a major in Business Management and an emphasis in accounting.

- In 2014 she became an Ordained Minister of the Gospel and receive her Honorable Doctorate at Abundant Harvest World Outreach Church under the leadership of Archbishop Effiong Noah who is now her husband in Africa Nigeria.
- In 2021 Graduate of Birthing The Dreams with K.A.G (Dr. Kishma George) Online Master Classes Purpose Pusher.

The journey started when she began to reach out to women in the Douglas County Jail Center. Washington State Prison, Atlanta Union Mission, and other Shelters throughout Metro Atlanta GA. She went on to receive what she called **"boot camp training"** through World Changers Ministry under the leadership of Dr. Creflo and Taffi Dollar. There she served as the Asst. Director over the Soul Winning Ministry.

Then led by the Spirit of God in 2008 she continued her training at Covenant Church of Jesus Christ in Macon GA for three years under the leadership of Overseer Angela Pitts. During her time of serving at CCOJC she received "Servant of the Lord" Award for her accomplishments in leadership, dedicated, faithful, and committed to the Kingdom of God. From there she went on to do outreach ministry in her hometown Cordele GA in 2010 and continues. Through the power of the Holy Spirit uncountable souls have been won to the Kingdom of God through her ministry gifts.

Websites:

https://tamikebrownministries.com/
https://outreachintfound.com/
https://dywtamike.com/tkkj-va-production/
https://gafvntv.org/gafv-roku-tv/

CHAPTER 1

Called Out to Lead Brings Separation

Dr. Tamike Brown

When God is ready to take your leadership abilities to the next level, He calls you out. You can no longer fit in a circle or a crowd. He will begin to empower you to lead. You are in transition to step up to leadership. It is not to say that you are better than anyone else it is because He has chosen you for a particular assignment and you answered the called. And the call requires you to separate from the circles and the crowds. You no longer fit in the circle because it is too tight for you now. There is no room for expansion, there is no room to grow, and there is no room to lead.

As a leader there must be a separation from certain things and many people. You may be thinking how I can lead if I am to separate myself from people. I will explain further in this chapter. God calls you to this assignment for a particular reason. And with the assignment everybody cannot go with you because as a leader God will begin to speak to you and show you things on another level that the circle or crowd will not understand. And it is your responsibility as a leader to consult God about everything not the crowd. God will give you guidance, directions, and instructions on how to lead. When you refuse to consult the Father, you will find yourself pleasing people verse pleasing God. As a result, you are no longer being led by Spirit of God; it is the blind leading the blind going nowhere.

When God calls you out to lead you will feel lonely at times. You will feel like you are all by yourself. You will feel like no one understands. And unbelievably they do not understand. When you accept the assignment to lead you are saying to God, I understand the road may feel lonely; however, I choose the lonely road if it means being obedient the Will of God for my life which is a part of God's Master Plan for humanity. You must choose to be alone if you are going to be a World Changer. Being alone you will discover who you are in Christ and who Christ is in you. Every great leader finds their true self when they were alone. And I am a witness. When God told me He was calling me out and that I no longer fit in I begin to discover things about me that I never knew exists.

When you are called out to lead you will be persecuted and crucified as to the people you look like you are not qualified. However, when God calls you to lead and not man, He appoint you, qualifies you, ordain you, anoint you, and seal it with His stamp of approval. Man will think you are not qualified because you are not leading according to the way they think you should lead. As a leader be willing to be led by the Spirit of God if you feel like you need assistant from someone while on the journey. No matter what, always be willing to consult God first. Man is full of opinions and suggestions.

I will quote this powerful statement from the ***Late Dr. Myles Munroe*** who once said "Whenever you decide to become yourself you become lonely. Because everyone around you wants you to be like them or they want you to become them. When you discover that you are unique, you are special, you are important, and you decide to become who you are, achieve the dreams and goals God has spoken and or shown to you, guess what? Lioness is the result of you becoming you.

What attracts people to you is when you decide you do not care if you are lonely; you are still going to pursue the vision to lead. ***When you use your lionesses properly, people will be drawn to you eventually***. A leader is always lonely because they are out front and there is no one out there with them. When you think about it, when you have everyone around you then you are part of the crowd. **When you pursue something more important than the crowd; you end up leading the crowd**" *Late Dr. Myles Munroe*

One of the biggest mistake leaders can make is trying to hold on to people that God is trying to disconnect you from. Trying to stay connected to a connection that God says disconnect could very well hinder your leadership ability to lead and grow. You must know what connections short term are, long term, or until Christ return. Everybody is not meant to stay connected to you until Christ return.

Godly Character is a high priority as a leader. You must govern your life according to the word of God and not according to your flesh. You must have self-control. It is one of the fruits of the Spirit God has given to us. You must spend quality time in the presence of God to get the directives from God to lead. Moses was considered a great leader in leading the people of God out of Egypt. But one day Moses decided not to obey the instructions from God instead he allowed the noise around him to get him in the flesh which interrupted the plan of God for his life. As many are familiar with the story God told Moses you will see the promise, but you will not enter. Now that is a disappointing thing to lead the people for many years and yet not being able to enter the promise land because you cannot control your flesh. You must be willing to exercise self-control.

When God calls you out of the circle or out of the crowd to lead you become God's property as He is allowing you to see the vision more clearly. It is hard to see the vision clearly when you are stuck in a circle around a lot of doubting and unbelieving people. You must be able to hear from God clearly. Everybody whispering in your ear can clog your spiritual ears and your ability to hear from God Himself. Stuck in a crowd will cause you to hear strange voices verse the voice of the Lord. And as a result, you are no longer being led by the spirit of God instead the crowd is leading you.

Back to the question as to how can you lead if you are not to be part of the crowd? I am reminded of a quote by ***James Crook once said, "A man who wants to lead the orc? must turn his back on the crowd."*** You cannot lead an orchestrate unless you turn your back to the crowd. If you are going to be a leader you must turn your back to the crowd. When you think about that quote it makes so much sense! It says it all. Pause be imaginative and think about that scenario. You are leading and for you to lead the crowd you must turn your back to the crowd. You are "Called Out" God has separated you from the crowd for you to lead the crowd. When you turn your back to the crowd the crowd is following you.

You must be willing to allow God to call you out to lead even if it may cause you to lose friends and or family members. Your top priority is to please God. That is a price to pay to lead. You will be misunderstood; friends walk away and so forth. Your mind must be **determined** to do God's Will no matter what life changes and challenges it brings. God will not let you fall when you accept the call.

Over the years I used to hear great men and women of God say sometimes you will feel like you will have to walk this walk alone because everybody is not going to understand the journey. I never understood what they meant at that time until I accepted the called. Although you may feel like you are alone, but you must know that you are not along because God is right there with you to carry you all the way through. Do not be afraid to answer the call when God calls you out of the circle or the crowd to lead. It has purpose. Trying to lead in a tight space will lead to self-destructions.

God had to pull Jesus out of the crowd for Jesus to lead the crowd and accomplish the will of God in the earth in being the Savior of the world by taking the sin penalty for humanity, which is why sin doesn't send people to hades or that dark place, but when a person rejects the works of Christ when He died for their sins. Christ maintained his character and fulfilled the Will of God for His life who set the example as a role model and a Powerful Leader to ever walk this earth.

A leader cannot go against the principles of God by doing wicked things. He is a righteous God and a righteous judge meaning you will be judge for the wicked things you do. Trying to accomplish a God given assignment without God will land you flat on your back because you are misleading God's people.

Integrity is a high priority as a leader. Doing wicked things just to make yourself look good as a leader or trying to make it to the top without God will get you in a world of trouble with God. 1 Peter 5:6 says to humble yourselves therefore under the mighty hand of God that He may exalt you in time. There have been great men of God who practiced wickedness while in leadership and landed flat on their backs because they love the power more than the power source who is God Almighty! Wickedness is a misrepresentation of the power of God Himself. The world today is in so much confusion and chaos due to wickedness.

Remember, if it feels like you do not fit in anymore; it is because you do not. God is separating you. You have been called out to lead.

ABOUT THE LEADER

Prophet Joshua Desousa

Joshua De Sousa is from Orange, New Jersey, he is a ghostwriter, preacher, and author who has been spreading the Gospel for over 11 years since the age of fourteen. He is the owner of a writing ministry and business, Sousa Scribal Solutions, where many have benefited from his visionary skill set as a ghostwriter, writing coach, and the founder of the Supernatural Scribes Writing Conference and the Invisible Impact Ghostwriting Academy.

CHAPTER 2

What Is in Your Hand?

Prophet Joshua De Sousa

In the third and fourth book of Exodus, there is a man by the name of Moses. When you ger a chance, read these two chapters in full, for you will see a lot of yourself in him. He was a humble man who has grown old in age after having to run away from his home after one of the worst mistakes of his entire life. Back home in Egypt, he accidentally murdered someone who was harming a Hebrew slave, because the dormant leader in him felt the burden to protect them.

He found himself far away in the wilderness so that he would not be found and safe from death, and he was trained on how to work as a shepherd. He became so content in his new home, far removed from the trauma of his past and turmoil of his people. Little did he know that God was about to interrupt his daily schedule.

One of his sheep would run all the way to a nearby mountain, and Moses had to chase them before they fell off or got mauled by another animal. As he looks for the sheep, he walks by a small cave or space within the mountain that has an unusual sight: a small tree that is surrounded by fire. Somehow, it is not burning, nor does it smell like smoke.

Before Moses could walk away, the tree would call his name, for God used this burning bush to show Moses His unusual and miraculous power. God would tell him that he is being chosen to go back to the same place he ran away from so that he can lead the Hebrews out of bondage, but of course, he would debate the Lord with endless excuses as to why it could never be him. The main excuse that most of us relate to was when he tells God that he could not speak eloquently. I know exactly how Moses felt, because I know what it is like to feel disqualified from your destiny

Growing up, I suffered quite a bit with depression, anxiety, and low-self-esteem due to my many insecurities. This includes being overweight, much darker than most of my black family and friends and struggling to talk. Even though I do not really stutter much, I stumble all my words all the time and have a challenging time articulating when I do not write things out beforehand. I used to hate preaching and teaching without a written sermon for this main reason, for I was afraid of being looked at as illiterate and unqualified.

To top things off, from the years of 2016 to 2020, I was unemployed, I got kicked out of college after failing the easiest major they offered which was a bachelor's degree in Youth Ministry. Lastly, I wanted to be officially ordained as a minister and prophet since I was thirteen, but I went through an endless cycle of abusive and controlling pastors who made me question my worth and value and tried to make me a clone of themselves.

Like Moses, after being kicked out of school, hiding from an old group of churches, and being without a job, I hid in my bedroom and in my suffering, believing that God abandoned me and that I was worthless like many said I was. I still mindlessly served at the church I found myself in, paid my tithes, and went to so many different conferences to keep my mind at peace. Then, in 2019, the Lord would ask me the same question that He asked Moses through the burning bush. Amid all of Moses' excuses, God stopped him and asked, "What is in your hand." Moses had a simple wooden staff, but God saw much more.

God told Moses to throw the staff down, and then it turned into a snake. God then told a fearful Moses to pick the snake up by the tail, and it became a staff again. He promised Moses that the same staff used to shepherd sheep would now be used as his sword, severing the Egyptians' grip on the Hebrews. Can it be that the gift or dream that you are afraid or ashamed to use is more powerful than you can ever imagine?

God reminded me of my calling to ministry. Even though all I wanted was to preach and teach in a church setting, He told me to look deeper. He reminded me of the many prophecies I have been receiving since I was 16 years old about not only becoming a preacher, but also an author. Even in my dormant season when I was not preaching at all after running away from a group of churches that counted me out, He told me to no longer wait for a man or woman to call me to the forefront. When He asked me "What is in your hand," my answer was, "I do not have money, influence, a college degree, or ministry title. All I have left to my name is a pen and a desire to write." I made up in my mind that even if I would never get a chance to preach in a pulpit again, I was going to preach the gospel with my pen. Little did I know that my penmanship was going to birth my leadership.

In 2019, I would start writing by faith, making ten-day

devotionals, and selling them on social media and sending them to people's email. Fast forward to January 2020, I would get a phone call that changed the trajectory of my life. A preacher called me saying the Lord told them that I would help them finally finish their first book that tried to write for three years. Just like Moses, I bombarded God and this person with so many excuses, including failing at college, not ever writing a full book yet, and simply not feeling worthy. After I saw my excuses would not let them change their mind, I took a deep breath and told God if He thinks I can do this, I will trust Him. Long story short, their book was released in October 2020. Being able to help them write their testimony resulted in hundreds of young people being encouraged and inspired by her book, showing me that even secretly, I was truly more inspirational and impactful than I could ever fathom.

When the coronavirus pandemic started in March of 2020, I did something that was prophesied over me just in August of 2019, that I would one day teach writing classes. Once again, I had no clue what I was doing, for I was still ghostwriting my first client's book and writing my first published book as well. I felt like I could not be taken seriously if I am teaching about writing if I did not have my first book out. I did not have any money or resources still, just my phone, Facebook Live, and burden to help other writers the same way I was helping my first client. Somehow, God allowed my very first conference, Supernatural Scribes, be filled with over 120 registrants who either watched the classes live or caught the replays. Even without a job, title, or degreed, dozens trusted me to pour into them and give them God-inspired strategies to finally finish that book that has been in their hearts for many years. Between May 2020 and me writing this passage in February 2020, over thirty books have been written and released among myself and those who attended any of the classes!

So, in the same manner that you would read that Moses defied all odds and freed the Hebrews from the Egyptians, I too defied all the odds and suddenly found myself leading and training an army of kingdom writers! I went from having no job at all to now having four jobs, as an author, writing coach, ghostwriter, and now even a youth pastor even though I did not get my youth ministry degree! Years ago, I would always beg God to open doors for me to preach the gospel in a church setting, which I know is still on the way.

However, I never thought my kingdom assignment would consist of helping dozens of believers, pastors, prophets, apostles, and entrepreneurs share their stories, wisdom, and scriptural insights. Even though I do not get credit for ghostwriting, I can hold my head up high in humble confidence, because my very words are causing hundreds to be saved, healed, delivered, encouraged, and inspired. When God asks you what is in your hand, do not hide it. Hold that dream, vision, pen, microphone, ball, or instrument high to the sky, because there is a limitless leader inside of you!

ABOUT THE LEADER

Pauline Mendo

Ms. Pauline Tangono Mendo is the Founder & CEO Hanna House of Help International Ministries, PBM Enterprise, Inc., The Mendo Group LLC and Co-Founder of Write On LLC. Ms. Pauline Tangono Mendo is an entrepreneur, Philanthropist, Best Selling Author of the "30 Day Soul Reset", CO-Author of the Anthology of "Called to Intercede' 'A Book Collaboration Volume 1-8. Pauline Mendo made her very first television appearance on WATC 57

ATLANTA 57 "Prophetic Impact" as a special guest speaker. Pauline is a fearless and faithful servant in the kingdom of God. She comes equipped, trained, and is anointed as an evangelist, preacher, prayer warrior, intercessor, teacher, missionary, psalmist, a prophetic worshipper, and a deliverance minister. Pauline Mendo is a traveling prophetic evangelist she has traveled and preached in various conferences, Tent revivals, open crusades in Kenya, Uganda, South Africa, and Puerto Rico and as a servant in the kingdom of God. Pauline is an active member and an ordained Evangelist at her current church home as a Servant Leader at Action Chapel Virginia, under the Leadership of the Presiding Dr. Bishop Kibby and First Lady Elsie Otoo.

CHAPTER 3

A Natural Born Leader

Evangelist Pauline Mendo

When I think of the saying, a natural born leader! We think of Harriet Tubman, Nelson Mandela, Mohandas Karamchand Gandhi, Martin Luther King, Joan of Arc, Malcolm X and Obama! Each leader I mention were history makers. They were recognized for their leadership and accomplishment to improve humanity. One that is called to lead is born to lead from conception. What does it mean to be a natural born leader? Natural born leaders are people with an innate capacity to effectively manage and lead groups of people to achieve collective goals. Instead of learning to become an effective leader, they have the instinctive ability to inspire others and encourage them to follow their vision.

When I recall the life of Harriet Tubman born a slave, but God called her to set the slaves free. She created the underground railroad. According to Wikipedia Harriet Tubman escaped and subsequently made some thirteen missions to rescue approximately seventy enslaved people, including family and friends, using the network of antislavery activists and safe houses known as the

Underground Railroad. She was nicknamed Moses! According to the Torah, the name "Moses" comes from the Hebrew verb, meaning "to pull out/draw out" [of water], and the infant Moses was given this name by Pharaoh's daughter after she rescued him from the Nile (Exodus 2:10).

Moses in the bible was a natural born leader as recorded in the scriptures. Moses was raised up to be "The Deliver" of the children of Israel from Egypt. The Bible says that when Moses was **eighty**, he was living peacefully as a shepherd in the desert. One day, as he was tending his flock, he heard the voice of God coming from a burning bush. God ordered Moses to go and force the Pharaoh to let his Hebrew people go. God took his time to develop Moses to deliver the millions of Israelites into the land of milk and honey.

When you think of a natural born leader there is an understanding that the leader must possess certain instinctive characteristics. I have chosen to use Moses as an example as a biblical leader because he successfully led the children of Israel out of Egypt; they consisted of about 2.5 to 3.0 million people. He led them through the wilderness for forty years and led them to the land of Canaan although he could not go into the land himself. He also wrote the first five books of the bible called the Pentateuch. He parted the red sea for the children of Israel to cross over. He also saw the backside of God. He wrote the ten commandments as directed by God Himself. He completed his assignment. Moses was an impeccable leader, and his remarkable leadership skill led the children of Israel on numerous wins and victories. The leadership qualities that Moses possesses made him an overnight success. It is imperative that we develop leadership skills and possess the qualities to be a successful leader.

Below are the characteristics found in the character of Moses that attributed to his success as leader.

They can be used as a guide for new emerging leaders:

Eager to Learn	Transparency
Active listening Trust	Innovation Accountability
Collaboration	Optimism
Courage	Passion
Communication	Patience
Empathy	Problem Solver
Flexibility	Resilience
Focus Growth mindset	Respect Self-Awareness

Every successful leader can improve their leadership skills and qualities by following the tips:

1. Identify your leadership style

Define how you want to lead your church, team, projects, or organization. Most professionals develop their own style of leadership based on factors like life experience and personality, as well as the unique needs of its organizational culture.

2. Define areas of strength and areas for improvement

Take time to consider which qualities you already have, and which offer opportunities to improve. Asking for professional feedback from trusted colleagues or mentors can help you identify strengths and weaknesses you might have missed. When we look at Moses, he was successful but one of his downfalls was his temperament. He had a bad temper.

Moses killed an Egyptian soldier and fled the country. He also became so angry at the people when God instructed him to speak to the rock and he struck the rock instead of speaking to it and that was the final straw for God. He told him that because he did not do what he was instructed to do because of his bad temper he would not be able to go into the land of Canaan, but he would see it. Moses needed to work on his temperament because it cost him his reward of entering the promised land. So, there is always room for improvement. Self-assessments are a good place to start as well as it will give you a more honest assessment of areas in which you can improve.

3. Find a mentor

Identify a person who you feel is a great leader or is a success that is an interest to you that will help you to be a success. Ask them to be your mentor. One way to connect with someone that is already a successful leader is to set up a time to meet and conduct a brief interview with them. You compile a list of five to ten questions you can ask them that contributed to their success. Use the opportunity to gain experience from them and adopt the qualities that make them successful.

4. Be patient

Becoming an effective leader can take time and becoming a protege to a leader that is already in interest is a fantastic way to becoming a successful leader as well. It takes time, months, years sometimes decades to become the natural born leader you are called to be. Joshua was Moses' protege and served him for over forty years before Jehovah appointed him to lead the Israelites in removing the Canaanites from the Promised Land. So, at that time he must have been at least 60 years old or olde. Some people dedicate their entire lives to becoming successful leaders. Be patient and allow yourself to make mistakes, learn from them and improve over time. Glean from the leaders that you serve as well will make you extremely polished as a leader.

ABOUT THE LEADER

Meri Horton

Charles and Meri Horton, Founders of Mission Possible Institute, have coached married and engaged couples for over 15 years. They are enthusiastic about helping couples achieve successful marriages and watching their families prosper. As certified facilitators in Saving Your Marriage Before It Starts (SYMBIS) assessments, Horton's work with engaged couples before they get married to help prepare them for lifelong love.

They are certified in Marriage on the Rock counseling to help couples succeed in a thriving and passionate marriage and Certified Mental health Coach with Light University.

The Horton's have experience in:

- couples coaching,
- family coaching,
- one-on-one coaching,
- webinars,
- workshops

Charles and his wife, Meri, have been married for over 29 years and are still romantically in love. They are the proud parents of three children and two grandchildren.

CHAPTER 4

Co-Preneurs

Meri Horton

In 2007, my husband and I opened," *The Shappy Chic Boutique.*"

We explored our love for fashion and opened a women's boutique. The rest is history. We worked together happily ever after.

Well, not really, but hopefully some couple somewhere did, but it was not us.

One day, a friend stopped by the boutique to shop. I could tell from first glance, something was wrong. Just looking at her, she was not happy, and looked as if she was mad at herself,

The inner corners of her eyebrows were raised, eyelids loose, lip corners pulled down in a deadly frown. I wondered if she felt as bad as she looked. You know me *Merciful Meri,* I had to help.

So, I jumped up, turned on some upbeat, gospel music, and said, "Let's do this, girl." So, we sang, clapped and dance for a while.

Then I got started, I had her trying on unique styles of clothes, shoes, and more clothes,

We drank coffee, we talked, tried on more clothes, and dance some more. I even joined her in trying on clothes. I was having an exciting time and I could see her demeanor changing. She had a sparkle in her eyes and look like the gorgeous friend that I know. She looked stunning.

After three hours of shopping and talking, it was time to leave.

I meandered over to the register to ring up her purchase. She opened her purse to pay…I then heard MYSELF say, "Your money is no good here. This is on me. "I just could not charge her. I gave her everything for free and I felt good doing it. She left out skipping to her car looking so happy, that it made me happy. For *now*, anyway.

The ride homes. The ride home brought me to my senses. "Who does that?" I said aloud to myself. "Who gives hundreds of dollars' worth of merchandise away in this day and time?" The pandemic had almost closed the boutique. We have no employees, which is why I am in the store 24/7.

Upon arriving home, my husband greeted me at the door with a big old smile, saying, "So how much money did you bring home to Big PAPA today?" My face just dropped!

I was thinking to myself, how am I going to explain to him that hundreds of dollars of our inventory were gone. Not stolen or not damaged, but given away by me, AGAIN! After a long silence, he saw the look on my face and said, "Please don't tell me you blessed someone." He did not really mean it as he said it. He is a true man of God who loves blessing people, but this was not a first. He walked away and turned and said with a strong, stern voice, "This is a business!"

I was so disappointed in myself; I just want to make people happy. I just wanted to share what God had blessed us with. I thought to myself, but how are we going to pay the rent and buy more inventory? So, I realize this is not for me. I should not be at the store, but not at the register. My daughter came to work. But I never paid her, so she quit. I finally accepted that I needed to hire someone and that I am not good with money. Charles will oversee payroll and the books. I must stop trying to tell him how to manage the money. That is not my sweet spot. Remember there is a lot less money because I kept giving things away. I was not being a good steward of what God had given us.

I AM THE CREATIVE ONE! I am good at ordering the clothes, putting styles together, and designing the store. I know because my husband would try to come in and do all those things, but he was horrible at it, and it was no secret. Before now, we just argued about it

We brought our attitudes home and did not speak to each other. Something was WRONG! We did not know our place and needed to reassess the whole thing if we were going to have a successful business and successful marriage. We knew the latter was most important to God. So, we STOP, OBSERVED, PRAYED, and reassessed what was happening in our lives.

We learned the hard way to stay in our place, BUT we LEARNED!

We learned a lot about working together, and by the Grace of God, we made it. One of the greatest lessons is celebrating each other's talents and finding ways to use them effectively. He learned that I am good at design, and foreseeing what something will look like in my head when completed. His strength is in business:

forecasting sales, compiling data, communicating strategic plans of what we need to do financially.

We combined our strengths and produce one of the most well-known companies in the industry today. Not as a boutique, but our coaching business.

When we stopped, observed, and prayed, we learned that we both would rather focus on a different business. We wanted to help people help themselves via personal coaching. Understand that we had to use our words better with each other and acknowledge our strengths and challenges using them properly in this new business.

The revelations and changes have made a tremendous difference in how the company is managed. It has also made a difference in our discussions at home.

Working together as a couple can be frustrating or great. You must decide which you want. It should be an easy question, but the most convicting question is, "Are BOTH of you willing to do the work?" Not so much the practical work of the business, but the practical work of the relationship.

Will you communicate and work to delegate those things that are not your sweet spot? Our advice for couples in business together is exercise patience. "Do not sweat the insignificant things. Most importantly, do not forget to take time for each other. Dinner, movie nights, even just a walk at the mall. DO NOT discuss business, this is a time to connect and reflect on your relationship and how far you have come as a couple.

Going into business with a spouse is like another marriage, you need to work in tandem to produce the best outcome possible."

Ecclesiastes 4:9-12 - Two [are] better than one, because they have a good reward for their labour.

Proverbs 27:17 - Iron sharpeneth iron; so, a man sharpeneth the countenance of his friend.

ABOUT THE LEADER

Elder Ivy Caldwell

Ivy Caldwell is the Owner of Footprint Enterprises, LLC which serves those who are ready to confront their past or present emotional trauma head-on and be healed through her Signature Coaching Program "Stepping Into ANEW You." If you are ready to move forward with your life, to get unstuck, to get your voice and authority back you can contact her through her website https://footprintenterprisesllc.com to set up a meeting.

Called to Lead Volume 1 An Anthology of Prolific Leadership
Dr. Monique Rodgers

She is a wife, mother, grandmother, fifteen times author, speaker, an ordained elder, a certified life coach, Christian counselor, TV, and podcast host. She has been serving in ministry for over twenty-five years. She is the author of "Expose It" which is her testimony of overcoming childhood abuse. Go ahead and expose your truth so you can be healed.

CHAPTER 5

Leaders Lead by Example

Elder Ivy Caldwell

When you say that God has called you and you become a Leader you are now under a microscope because people will be watching you. They are not watching you to see if you fall or make a mistake. They are watching you to see if you believe what you preach. Our actions carry more weight when we are in ministry. As leaders we should not teach and preach to the people the way of life and we are not living it. We are to be living examples of how to walk out this life.

As an Elder, I have been allowed to learn, grow, watch, given grace to make mistakes, and to put into action what I have been taught. I have been trained in all areas of ministry. I have been assessed, tried, and I am trusted to lead others. At a moment's notice I could be called upon to fill in for any ministry function where there is a need; except; for the singing ministry. That is not my lane. If necessary, now I can make a joyful noise unto the Lord. I hope you are smiling at that statement. As leaders, we are to use our gifts and talents in a way to be a blessing and not a burden. As a Leader, I have come to learn there are some principles we must have in place to be successful. We must lead by example and have the following attributes in our lives:

Mentorship: A mentor is someone who has many years of experience being in ministry and they are not a novice. None of us know it all! As a leader, you should have a mentor to teach and glean from. Someone who is above your level, and they are grounded in God's Word. There will be times when you are faced with a situation, and you will not know what to do. This is when you can call on your mentor to get wisdom and knowledge from them as they share their experiences with you. Your mentor is someone who has insight and the keen ability to get to the root of the issue. They will help you to gain perspective and how to oversee situations.

Accountability: You always want to have someone in your life that you are accountable to and that will hold your feet to the fire. As a leader, you should have someone in your circle that you are accountable to because this keeps you honest. If you need to have your accountability partner to bring something to your attention this person should feel comfortable enough to do so. You want someone in your life that will support, encourage, and correct you. You will not be offended when they bring something to your attention about what you need to correct or change. You will be grateful for them being in your life and not allowing you to go the wrong way. Many leaders fall because they do not allow others to check them, and this leads to pride. We do not want to ever think so highly of ourselves that no one can tell us anything. If I love, you I will tell you the truth and not allow you to go the wrong way.

Ask for Help: Do not be stuck on stupid. If you know you do not know how to do something do not be so prideful that you do not ask for help. No one knows it all or has it all. "And He Himself gave some to be apostles, some prophets, some evangelists, and some pastors and teachers, for the equipping of the saints for the work of ministry, for the edifying of the body of Christ, till we all come to the unity of the faith and of the knowledge of the Son of God, to a perfect man, to the measure of the stature of the fullness of Christ;" (Ephesians 4:11-13) God has put many gifts in the Body so use them because you don't have all of them. We are interdependent upon one another.

Character and Integrity: Character is what you do when no one is looking. I say, "My character does not change no matter where I am." Your character will take you where your gift will not. When the time is right your gift will make room for you. Do not be one way at church and another way at home. We must always live this life no matter where we are. Do not have a different face for those you encounter, and we must be always consistent.

Your Words: Your words have power and can shape lives. Be a person of your word. People cling to the words we say. If you say that you are going to do something, then do it. Do not say you can do something, and you cannot. People have been lied to so much in their lives that it is hard for them to trust or believe in Church Leadership. We do not want to give leadership a bad name. If you cannot do something, be man or woman enough to say so. As soon as you find out that you cannot let them know. People will get leery of someone who cannot keep the word. They will respect you for being honest.

It is okay to say no because you are unable to do a request. It is okay to have an off day but not all the time. It is okay not to feel well because we are in a human body that gets weary, tired, and sick; so, take care of yourself. It is okay to take a break; even Jesus went away to rest, relax, and get in a quiet place to be with his Father. If you have these attributes in place in your life to keep you from going off track, you will have set yourself up for success in your ministry as you lead.

ABOUT THE LEADER

Rhonda P. Fraser

Rhonda P. Fraser is a global women's leader who considers her Christian Faith paramount. She has been married to Rev. Reginald Fraser since 1988 and together they have three beautiful children.

She is an empowerment specialist, inspirational speaker, personal development/leadership coach and functions in women's leadership/advisory roles for several organizations, including churches, mostly in New York.

Rhonda co-authored seven books including this one. She is a bestselling author for the following inspirational books:

1. Resilient Faith: Dare to Believe (Lead Author and Compiler)
2. Women of War: Peace in the Midst of Storm (Co-Author)
3. This is How I Fight My Battles (Co-Author)
4. Called to Intercede (Co-Author)

Her 2022 new release book is "Empowered to Overcome Tough Seasons of Life"

Rhonda is an accomplished Corporate Finance, Marketing and Strategy Expert, with a master's degree (MBA) from Villanova University.

She has been featured on FOX, CBS, and NBC news and on various billboards.

Websites To Connect with Rhonda Fraser:

www.rfraserconsulting.com
Rhondafraser.com
Facebook: Rhonda P. Fraser
Instagram: @rhondapfraser

CHAPTER 6

Wisdom and Balanced Leadership

RHONDA FRASER

Most people will lead or influence someone at some point in life, whether large groups of people, a smaller team, our family or, at least, our own life. In a world of blame-shifting, it is important to remember that the Bible indicates in Romans 14:12 that we must give an account to God for how we lead our lives. That means taking responsibility for the thoughts we entertain and actions we take. That is ultimate leadership! Therefore, I believe this chapter will resonate with everyone, whether you think you are called to lead millions of people or just one person. Leadership has its rewards and responsibilities. To focus primarily on the benefits and lose sight of the obligation of headship is irresponsible. Equally to lose our joy over the required accountability is futile. Consequently, finding the correct equilibrium is vital. Christian leadership is outstanding because we get to demonstrate the attributes of management, including servant leadership, and using godly wisdom - knowing how, when, and where to apply the necessary knowledge. It means functioning with more than intellect and skillset; it entails relying on divine input. We get the added advantage of direction from the omnipotent and omnipresent One – our God who is all powerful, all knowing and ever-present. It is having His Holy Spirit guide us and experience His peace even when executing difficult and unexpected decisions. To be trusted to handle anything of significance requires great wisdom. It is no wonder God granted Solomon wealth and all that comes with it because he asked for wisdom. It takes keen perception to conduct ironic decision-making and to find the right balance. Good leaders understand this poise very well. Jesus, our perfect role model, showed us how to manage this conflicting pendulum. Although, He was God in human form – the highest person to walk on earth - a man of great authority, He still demonstrated a servant leadership style and did not think it was beneath Him to engage with ordinary people. Therefore, the challenge of the leader is how to successfully balance our God-given authority and effectively connect with people. The following are some key considerations to wisely navigate the opposing sides of leadership. Prayer and faith should be supported with follow-up action. It is true that there are some dead-end situations where prayer and trusting God is the only resolve to the situation. However, we cannot be lazy in our approach to challenges and not act where needed. Although the Christian life is rooted in faith and prayer, the Bible reminds us in James 2:17 that faith without works is dead. Indeed, there is much power when we pray and intercede. That communion is literally our lifeline. We must pray against distractions and setbacks aimed at hindering us. Jesus was intentional in taking time to pray to His father. However, after He prayed, He frequently went into action. Prayer often boosts us into action. Many of us receive guidance during prayer for our next steps. I gave some important insight into the power of prayer and intercession in my chapter in the book, "Called to Intercede, Volume 1." It is important to hold firm to values while being open-minded about the varying methods of accomplishing responsibilities. A fitting example is with the thief on the cross who asked Jesus to remember him when He came into His Kingdom. Although, the Bible informs us in Mark 16:16 that "he who believes and is baptized will be saved", common sense tells us the thief had no opportunity to get off the cross to be baptized at that moment. Those who hold fast to certain rules and rituals would have denied this man access to eternal life because of his setback, but not Jesus. He said, "TODAY, you will be with me in paradise." Jesus is always ready to respond to authentic cries for salvation and help. I believe after reading this book, some people will experience His urgent response to their desperate cry, and He may very well show up in an unconventional way. Leaders are expected to be decisive, independent thinkers yet encourage teamwork and feedback.

The challenge is knowing when to embrace solitude and when to include others. When we step away from the chaos, we get to hear, both our thoughts, and God's voice clearer. Most of the major

projects I undertook, were done during a time of solitude. I particularly remember co-authoring most of my books in the heart of the pandemic. It was a time of shut-in from the noise and distraction to refocus on the call to fulfill the assignment. However, the book collaborations also included input from other authors – sharing with others. We cannot accomplish our God-given assignment on our own. Leadership requires the acknowledgement that support is necessary and knowing the timing of boldly embracing that relationship. Jesus chose twelve imperfect men from all levels of society and patiently guided them to conduct His mission when He left. All those disciples, except for one, were able to eventually execute that mission and we are recipients of the baton that was passed on throughout the ages. It is important to note that although Jesus knew Judas would betray Him and walk away, our Master still included him. The betrayal did not affect Jesus' mission – it propelled Him towards it. What a great lesson in leadership! We cannot allow those who disregard our value to shake our faith in connecting with others or derail our God-given purpose. Leadership may come with the privilege of sitting in the office with direct reports, but it also requires getting on the battlefield when needed. Jesus journeyed with His team, showing them the way. They saw firsthand how he handled various situations and His guidance gave them confidence to do the same when He left earth. A good leader understands how to develop others through many forms like training, correction, commendation but demonstration is always impactful. As a strategic leader, I fully understand the importance of grasping opportunities, mitigating risks, utilizing strengths, and developing the weaknesses. However, Christian leadership requires more than the ability to identify and utilize knowledgeable, skillful, and experienced people and naturally resourceful opportunities. It is also having the wisdom to discern God is called out ones – His anointed ones. That is the wisdom Prophet Samuel displayed when he anointed the young shepherd boy, David, to become the next King, much to the disbelief of even the boy's own father. However, timing is important. David did not become King at the time of his anointing; it took some time. Doing the right thing at the wrong time or in the wrong place could have negative consequences. Leadership requires the knowledge of when to stay in position and when to move. To stay in a place where your assignment is over could result in diminishing returns. Leadership also means knowing when to be silent and when to speak up. Learning to pick battles is essential. Some hurting people project their hurt onto others. They do not necessarily want solutions; others truly need help. This is the scenario that was displayed with the two thieves on the cross. One attacked and mocked Jesus' power. The other one understood that, although Jesus was in a difficult part of His journey, He still had authority to transform lives. That man embraced Jesus' power and received what he requested. True leaders never have to engage in unnecessary disputes or force anyone to see their value. Authentic leaders with healthy self-worth never have to exaggerate or dull their shine for acceptance. Christ gives us true self-worth. Low self-esteem fuels insecurity, envy, and jealousy. It leads to stagnation, defamation, and harm to others. Exaggerated esteem belittles others and is prideful which leads to downfall. Jesus exhibited His incredible knowledge at a youthful age in the temple alongside the religious leaders, yet he pursued the forgotten, neglected and rejected ones. He was never afraid of being misjudged or misunderstood. It is critical for leaders to know when to press through in faith, even in impossible situations and when to yield to God's plan, even if initially a different approach or outcome was preferred. We see Jesus doing the impossible like raising Lazarus from the dead, but we also see Him yielding to the torture that led up to His death on the cross. There are so many stories in my books, particularly my book Resilient Faith: Dare to Believe, where even doctors had discouraging prognosis for several people, including myself, but the nudging faith in our hearts caused us to press through and see miracles. On the contrary there are stories of others who believed God, hoping for a different result, yet it did not work out the way initially desired. In time God proved and continues to prove Romans 8:28, that "all things work together for good for those who love the Lord and are called according to His purpose." That is the wisdom that gives peace in every decision and its outcome, and that helps to bring the balance in leadership and life.

ABOUT THE LEADER

Prophetess Christine Ugbomah

Christine immigrated to the United States at an early age from the U. K. and comes from a large family who is very much into music and entertainment. She is a plural artist, poet, and author. Christine has self-published several of her books on Kindle and Amazon. Her passion is to lead, encourage and motivate the women she has been called to uplift by faith through her devotional journals, workbooks, coaching, and the arts. Christine loves to teach art and is always looking to implement her techniques in her work. Christine spends her time learning innovative approaches in the arts. Her work has been displayed in The Carnegie Museum for Art for her artwork in Photography: The August Wilson African American Cultural Center. Christine's art and her jewelry were displayed as well. Christine's powdered glasswork was displayed in the Pittsburgh Glass Center Gallery. Christine is always in school and is currently working on her bachelor's with hopes of becoming an art therapist soon, and her favorite color is blue.

CHAPTER 7

The Leadership Role Are You called to Lead?

Christine Ugbomah

It has been both my experience and training that there are several reasons why people become Leaders. Some leaders have been called by God, while others become leaders purely as a career. Those words were shocking to me since I am referring to those who have a charismatic air about them that their language is so persuasive that they tickle the listener's ears: no anointing, no call but impressive poise, and a flair for good taste in clothes. People flock to them and line up to feel good, and they do not require change, just a good word.

Then there is the Leader like Saul, who runs in the other direction like Saul did when the call came; he hid. Those indeed called to lead already have seen and heard enough to know that it can be a thankless job and that the attack on leaders is Real. The bible has countless leaders whose biographies make us question God at first until we understand God's methodology.

He calls the ones He has qualified. What I love about God is how he can download into a leader who has never gone to any traditional schools; they do not hold any degrees, yet God continuously keeps downloading revelation so profound that the people of influence stand or sit still to catch a word or two of that downloaded, that person who seem unqualified to us. SELAH.

According to Dr. Matthew Stevenson, "We lead ourselves first before we lead others." I was unaware of that fact because I grew up without both parents; I was clueless. That revelation gave me a sense of peace and, at the same time, showed me how God was the one who was grooming me to become His Leader. Leaders may very well be born, but all need instructions to lead well.

It is an honor to be called by God to lead. Whether I feel ready or not, I know without any doubt that He will never send me without processing me.

God loves His leaders as well, as He chastises them when they do not represent Him well. He loves us so much that He deals with us accordingly when we do not treat one another right. God is such a compassionate God. When we tell God our faults and issues as to why he cannot use us, He tells us why we can do what he has called us to do and that his view of our frailties is no surprise to him.

All designers and creators know what their products can produce and how they function. Our maker knows us through and through, and he has tested us up to this point and will continue to test his up-and-coming leaders well up to the day he installs them and beyond. He will sometimes send us help to complete an assignment that we could have done on our own just by showing up.

We tend to forget that when we show up, God is showing up! Leaders are called to represent someone, not necessarily ourselves.

As Ambassadors, we describe the Kingdom, not ourselves, and it is easy to forget this truth. I have seen Ambassadors upset because something said or done was considered an insult to the Kingdom, not the representative sitting at the table.

As a Leader, the art of prayer is a much-needed lifestyle. If a Leader does not have a prayer life that gives them an intimate relationship with God, they will always be at the mercy of gimmicks and tricks to lead people; All leaders receive the stamp of approval from God before they go out into ministry or the marketplace. When God sends you out as a leader, the instructions must be received and implemented to achieve success. Because He has already given you how to lead, if this is not the case, then that person can be starting their ministry too soon. It is dangerous, and well-meaning leaders may release them before their time. Even if the word of prophecy has been spoken over you, it is God's timing that matters the most. So, check to see if you are indeed called to lead others. Check with God who you are called to and where God has sent you. Beloved God gives instructions and strategies for where He has already called you to. God is a loving father; He has not called you to false starts. We need you whole and ready to lead us awesomely equipped and on fire, confidently executing your orders for the Kingdom of God. It is my prayer that you run well and that you run with faithful servants to hold up our hands as you move through everything your purpose calls you to with the fire of God in your mouth as u speak and preach the unadulterated word of God will keep you, God will always have your back

GO AND BE GREAT at it.

ABOUT THE LEADER

Dr. Monique L. rodgers

Dr. Monique Rodgers is an international bestselling author, CEO, visionary, master business coach, certified vegan health coach, motivational speaker, entrepreneur, educator, and literary genius. Dr. Rodgers excels today as a notable writing coach, founder, and serial entrepreneur. Throughout the course of her career, she has written such prolific works such as Hello! My name is Millennial. Picking up the Pieces, The Majestical Land of Twinville, Falling in

Love with Jesus, Accelerate, Overcoming Writer's Block, Just Breathe, Called to Intercede Volumes 1-7 and I am Black History. She has also been included as a co-author in collaborations such as Jumpstart Your Mind, Speak Up We Deserve to be Heard, Finding Joy in the Journey Volume 2, and Let the Kingdompreneurs Speak. Due to her outstanding breadth of experience, Dr. Rodgers has been featured on Rachel Speaks radio program, The Love Walk Podcast, The Glory Network, God's Glory Radio Show, The Miracle Zone, The Healing Zone, The Joyce Kiwani Adams Show, Coach Monique Ph.D. radio show, and many more. She has graced numerous platforms worldwide. She served as a TV host for WATCTV. She has been featured in Heart and Soul magazine, My Story the Magazine, and Kish Magazine's Top 20 Authors of 2021. She has also been featured in Marquis Who's Who in America 2021-2022. She also assisted in various volunteer work including an executive team member for Lady Deliverers Arise, Aniyah Space, and a board member for the I Am My Sister organization. She is also a certified master business coach, certified vegan health coach, and a health advocate. She has served in various leadership positions in business and in ministry. She is currently an Awakening Prayer hub leader for the city of Raleigh under the tutelage of Apostle Jennifer LeClaire. She is an ambassador for Kingdom Sniper Institute under the mentorship of Evangelist Latrice Ryan. As an expert in her field, Dr. Rodgers earned an undergraduate degree through Oral Roberts University as well as a Master of Science degree and a doctorate in global leadership through Colorado Technical University. She has also studied at The Black Business School online. Looking towards her future, Dr. Rodgers intends to expand upon her expertise and continue serving through ministry for God. She aspires to help over one hundred authors to complete and publish their books, help intercessors to draw closer to God and help train marketplace prophets and leaders for success.

Contact information:

www.getwriteoncoaching.com
Facebook: www.facebook.com/moniquerodgers2
Instagram: @drroyalty7
Twitter: @DrMonique7
LinkedIn: Dr. Monique Rodgers
YouTube: Dr. Monique Rodgers
Clubhouse: @DrMonique7
Email: calledtointerecede@gmail.com

CHAPTER 8

Leading With The Heart Of God

Dr. Monique Rodgers

The greatest teacher of all time for leadership was Jesus. He set the tone and modeled the mere essence of leadership to his disciples. He was very selective and strategic in his selection of leaders. Once of the most important keys that he held as a leader was that he had the heart of God. He was able to successfully lead his disciples with excellence because he loved God first and he loved each disciple. One of the most beautiful times that I have had in leadership is being able to pray and to seek the heart of God concerning issues that I have faced as a leader.

Leadership takes a lot of commitment, accountability as well as dedication to those we are leading. Some of the most value keys that I have learned as a leader is to listen to those that are following me. Listening in a manner to which I can hear the heart of what they are asking or needing. I have also learned the value of accountability in leadership. In Bible it states that in the multitude of counselors there is safety. I have been blessed to surround myself with leaders who also carry the heart of God in leadership. Another key element is the art of compassion. As a leader it is essential to care about others and to also have sympathy and empathy. There is nothing worse than serving a heartless leader that does not care about you or have compassion for your feelings. As leaders it is pertinent that we share the same compassion that Jesus shared.

When you are called to be a leader there are certain characteristics that will be unveiled through you to others. There is an ability to influence others as well as take charge without anyone asking. As a called leader you are also a natural born leader that can lead on vast levels. Whether you are leading in the marketplace, in the pulpit, in the classroom, in your home, in your marriage, in the board room, in the courtroom, in the barbershop, or nail shop there is a leader inside of that is hungering for more of God's heart as a leader. My prayer for you as leaders is that as you lead may you grow even closer to God and tap into his heart and discover the true needs of the people to which you are leading. Leading as a calling is a major responsibility that should never be handled lightly.

ABOUT THE LEADER

Prophetess Patricia Shirley

Patricia is a Dynamic Organizational Leader and top performer who thrives in fast-paced environments. Understands all employees must comprehend their roles and given room to grow, and that building the right organization is the foundation for building the right products and services. Elicits order from chaos with a prudent approach to building products and product teams. Strong ability to deliver by predicting and identifying key roadblocks. Dynamic leadership skills that engender buy-in and trust. Results-oriented problem solver. Track record of resolving complex issues in a consistent and reliable manner. Patricia Shirley is operations and management consultant, serial entrepreneur, speaker, educator, and published author versed in an array of industries, including healthcare, government, education, and startup enterprises. Patricia has directly invested over two decades in healthcare operational leadership. Patricia has been responsible for revenue cycle management, nonprofit management, program development, direct healthcare delivery systems, operational implementation, contract negotiations, software implementations, multi-site and facility mergers, training and development of staff, New York State licensed continuing education instructor. Founder of Patricia Shirley Enterprises, Shirley Academy, Destiny Decree Design, and her newest launch Boss Global360.

How to Contact:

Instagram: @pa_global360
Facebook: https://www.facebook.com/patricia.shirley.56027
Website: www.patriciashirley.com
https://beaconsai/pshirleyglobal
www.bossglobal360.com
Email: info@patriciashirley.com.

CHAPTER 9

Leadership Transitions

Patricia Shirley

We are amid one of the most significant transitions in American history. Economic insecurity, a post-pandemic world, unexplainable sickness and disease, and a slew of new processes and procedures to address these concerns. It almost looked like the Titanic as they boarded the ship, unaware that they were about to sink. Then sometimes we felt like Prince Charming was putting the shoe on Cinderella as a sort of exhale or pause to all the difficulty. Amongst these highs and lows, these challenging times served as a refinement to many leaders in the skill set many had become accustomed to. This unpredictable environment birthed "the transitional leader."

Which thrust us into this ready set and go environment. This has caused companies, businesses, and even the entire country to reconsider long-standing processes, employee jobs, skill set, and leadership skills required to handle a typical workday. It places an emphasis on "how we do business." Better yet, how we keep going amidst the myriad of changes? Leaders have been walking a tightrope for the past two years, attempting to maintain stability while dealing with a disruptive and unpredictable epidemic, battling to hire in the face of a 15- year high in talent shortages, and overhauling policies to meet employee expectations for more flexibility at work. This disruptive and ever-changing environment causes the transitional leader's quality and skill.

We are currently in a state of constant change and evolution. If we, as leaders, are indeed "called to lead" and, to varying degrees, called to transition. Companies, organizations, and environments we Must awaken to the transitional leadership abilities that lord on the inside of us. A transitional leader acts as a change agent to move the business, company, ministry, or project to the next stage of development.

They bring foresight, strategy, and solutions to situations of extreme insecurity. These transitional leaders navigate with ease the rough terrain because it is at the heart of their leadership abilities. Possessing an innate ability to ask specific questions and assess environments spiritually and naturally as they advance their business, family, and projects forward. Companies, organizations, and environments must awaken to the transitional leadership abilities that lord on the inside of us. One may ask why the need for a transitional leader? Well, when you explore the innate characteristics.

That they possess you see the dire need for these leadership characteristics. Transitional Leadership: Anticipates Failure Transitional leaders expect the failures that will result from their actions. Inherent risk takers who will accept full responsibility in the face of vehement opposition. They recognize the possibility of failure, but they also accept the level of risk required to propel the company, organization, and facilities to the next level of development.

They recognize successful leaders accept responsibility. Leaders who are successful accept responsibility for their failures. A leader's denial of fallibility or fault can only harm the organization's perception of the leader. Denial of fallibility contributes to a dysfunctional culture of unfairness and finger-pointing. The transitional leader is skilled at self-awareness.

Transitional Leadership: Pitfalls

- Advancing too quickly before receiving agreement and support from those on the team. • The ability to see the vision and have foresight while overlooking process steps that would cause better results. By skipping critical steps, the new system implementation may fall apart, forcing the team to restart from scratch. Transitional Leader: Benefits • Hindsight and foresight that others do not have. They are normally the ones with the vision that others do not see.
- Skilled in the school of "hardship and difficulty." They possess the ability to adapt more readily and quickly than others do. Making huge pivots that come with dynamic blessings, new opportunities, and additional income streams.
- What is cold or callouses to others is a mechanism within them to cut off dead weight and dead assignments. Once they see the alternative course of action, they immediately turn their focus and attention towards it, even at the risk of people not accepting. • Unconventional level of structure

and planning They can build strategic because of the constant shifting and changing. Fewer resources, but greater results. Because their planning comes from a variety of haphazard sources, this has now become their greatest strength.

ABOUT THE LEADER

Coach Krystal Henry

Krystal Henry is an author, motivational speaker, and success coach, who created “Made to Lead Millions,” a multi-dimensional book on leadership and a coaching hub, offering solutions, strategies, and inspiration to a diverse clientele. She is often known for her innate ability to lead others "from what if,” to “what is." Having overcome life-changing battles with covid, cancer, infertility, and much more. Krystal proves herself an unfeigned survivor, equipped to change lives, bringing about a "Believe Better" mindset. Krystal is the Leading Lady of Power of the Gospel Ministries, alongside her husband Pastor Redd. Together they inspire the masses, on the trailblazing "Power Lift Podcast" a part of the Positive Power XXI Christian Media.

Krystal is the author of inspirational manuscripts: "The Elements of You" and "Made to Lead Millions." She has also co-authored in "Jumpstart Your Mind," "Success Chronicles, Volume One. You Define Your Own Success" and "Let the Kingdomprenuer Speak," and "Called to Intercede" all organic expositions of an authentic passion, for people.

Krystal Henry. Leader. Speaker. Philanthropist.

CHAPTER 10

Leaders Defend

Coach Krystal Henry

Leaders defend. Leaders take on causes, reasons, and motivations to lead. Have you ever been told you need a cause, reason, or motivation to lead? I could not understand why there was a need for leaders to find fulfillment through defense. I am not a lawyer, in the army, a police officer, or firefighter, however as a leader I have been called to defend. Defense means safeguarding, yielding security, justification, endorsement, cover, vindication and shielding. Once I read the definition my eyes of my understanding began to open. Leaders defend the truth, morality, a team, equality, unfair treatment, and a company. Leaders take a stand when no one else will or can. Stepping up and out if difficult for many people and this is one of the reasons people choose to take the low ground instead of defending someone or something. Can you think of a time when you stood up for a cause? Have you ever experienced a time where you needed someone to stand up for you or with you?

There is power in numbers and power in support. Support is one of the most powerful things we can do to help someone. Even if you stand with someone in silence, just knowing you are there means so much to that person! I was asked to do a bible study for some college students. The series God gave me was called "Single & Set Apart." It was such a powerful move of God. Singles were bringing other singles to experience the mighty move. The bible study started with the topic a "Bite of Forbidden Fruit" with Adam and Eve. Then "The Tongue" that ignites a fire from the book of James and how conversations can take things beyond holiness was our second lesson. The incident of Dinah from Genesis 34: 2 which states, "And when Shechem the son of Hamor the Hivite, prince of the country, saw her, he took her and lay with her, and violated her." This HOT topic brought a cause and purpose to surface, as the third lesson.

There was a young man that began to wrench his hands after the scripture was read and the teaching began to ensue. Dinah was trespassed against! Trespassing is a violation, encroachment, intrusion, invasion, or infringement of your privacy, body, mind, soul, and property. Once the definition was given the young man's hand quickly went up. I asked him if he had a question. He said, "he had a dilemma and did not know how to manage the situation." He said, "it involved the sexual assault of his friend." She said, she did not want to tell the police or anyone but him. Her embarrassment and shame were too great to go through everything with people she did not trust.

Students in the room began to chime in. Some said, "she needs to tell, others said if it were them, they would remain silent." Others wanted to know who, when, where, why, and how. Were they in the room now? Finally, I hushed the group and slowly explained to the young man who started it all. As a survivor of sexual assault, I did not tell. I explained I was drugged by a friend who I had known for years and trusted. I had not been drinking the night it occurred. I went to hang out and play cards. I remember waking up with my face on the kitchen table, crying in a bed, and finding myself completely naked the next day. Confused. Bewildered. Time missing! At, a complete loss. My friend casually said, "Good Morning!" I asked what happened? He said, I got wild last night and asked me what did I take? Take? I did not drink or take anything? He had everything all thought out. It was his words against my missing time. So, I went home and did not say a word.

The room remained silent for a minute or so after I finished telling them my experience. They were not expecting me to tell them my experience. Then I stated that, 1 in 6 women have been raped or experienced an attempted rape in America in their lifetime. The percentage of rapist that are caught, convicted, and go to jail are too low to count as a real defense of women in America. I had a cause but remained silent, because of shame, embarrassment, fear, doubt, and evidential issues.

The day of that Bible Study was the day I broke my silence. I realized that the guilty, the assailant, the predator, or perpetrator want us to remain silent. That was the day I began to deal with the nightmares and lost time. How many of Dinah are out there in silence and who will stand with HER?

When you become a leader, you also become a defender. It is up to you to choose the cause, reason, and motivation that you wish to spearhead. Let your passion led you to lead others out of shame, silence, fear, doubt, failure, loss, and a cause that you can make a difference with.

I encourage you to do not be silenced or remain silent, stand up for yourself and others. There is power in numbers, support, the truth, and breaking the Silence!

ABOUT THE LEADER

Stephannie Green

Stephannie Green is the Founder and CEO of Power Wealth Profits LLC® Founder of Heritage Faith Ministries.

She is a two-time #1 Amazon Best Selling Author and mentioned on over four hundred media outlets. As well as a Licensed Evangelist, Intercessor, Certified Master Business Coach, Wealth Builder, Licensed in Life & Health, Thought Leader, Financial Literacy Strategist and Speaker.

She educates and transforms lives on living off residual Passive Income.

She is a wife, mother, and friend.

Stephannie Green Empowers Women to Prosper according to Deuteronomy 8:18. Women assuredly, need to have their own personal Health & Wealth. Oftentimes women rely on men and have never really handled the household finances. It is a New Day for Your Life Reimagined, Investing and being Wealthy & Healthy.

Contact Information

Powerwealthprofits.com
Sgreen@powerwealthprofits.com
Facebook.com/StephannieGreen
Instagram.com/G._Stephannie

CHAPTER 11

Are You a Visionary?

Evangelist Stephannie Green

In the Bible King Solomon stated,

"Where there is no vision, the people perish: but he that keepeth the law, happy is he." (Proverbs 29:18 KJV – King James Version)

Let us review this in another translation.

(The NIV- New International Version)

"Where there is no revelation, people cast off restraint; but blessed is the one who heeds wisdom's instruction."

Greetings my friend! I am super excited that you are reading the words in this chapter of the anthology entitled, **Called to Lead** – Chapter 11 ***"Are You a Visionary*?"** Well, if the answer is YES, you are Absolutely in the right place, at the right time! I would like to share the definition of the word vision with you, as it is defined in the Merriam-Webster dictionary, affirming; "**The act of power of imagination**. "

Wow! There's power in our **imaginations**. As a visionary, we see things in a vision that has not yet appeared unto others. This can be challenging at times, considering, it may seem to become a very lonely space due to others may not understand your vision. The reason being, when the **vision is for you to see in your heart and mind**, others cannot see, whatever you are seeing. However, be encouraged as it relates to (Habakkuk 2:2 KJV) "*And the Lord answered me, and said, Write the vision, and make it plain upon tables, that he may run that readeth it.*" This is extremely vital when leading others. "Keep in mind, that vision is a function of the heart, and sight is a function of the eyes. There is no greater source of hope and confidence than that of vision. It is the key to unity, a magnet for commitment, and the motivational stimulus for personal and corporate discipline and growth." And remember, patience is a virtue for everything to come together.

Have you ever considered starting a business? One of the first businesses I created was an Adult Care Home. It requires state licensing, as well as continuing education credits. It also demands planning ahead (foreseeing the future). In addition, it is essential for placing people, strategically in their proper positions. Vision is not limited to exclusively starting a business, regardless of age.

Here is a list of potential areas of vision:

1. Creating an App, or invention that will solve a problem in society (Thomas Edison Invented the Light bulb)
2. Physical Fitness (Physically, Emotionally & Mentally) - Staying hydrated
3. Work, Business or Career (Like the Wright Brothers inventing the airplane)
4. Relationships (Being whole individually and collectively

1 x 1 = 1)

5. Healthy Finances (God will provide open door opportunities when you have a strong, deep-down desire)
6. Spiritual Life and Belief (Higher Frequencies & Believing God for it)
7. Contributions to Yourself and Serving others (Give and it shall be given to you)
8. Writing Your Vision in the PRESENT tense (Visualize yourself genuinely being there, elevated NOW)
9. Living a Life of Excellence and Significance (Confident in who you are, and knowing the Value you bring to helping others, yet guarding your heart)
10. Pursuing Your Dreams (Thinking and acting; DREAM BIG unapologetically)
11. Writing a Book, Daily Affirmations or Songs (Use a Journal to write the plan)
12. Learning something NEW (Developing your Talents, passion and remaining positive)
13. Start a list of things…" *Where there is no vision, the people perish*" (Proverbs 29:18 KJV)

As a visionary, we are on the front line. This is the area where the enemy tries to steal, kill, and destroy the blessings on the other side of the vision. It comes in many forms, such as trying to discourage the visionary, being offended by someone, or unexpectedly not forgiving someone. Nevertheless, continue to implement processes, believing, pressing forward, and flying high like an eagle. Eagles Soar High in the Sky, consequently, the enemy will flee and fail, since he cannot survive in the environment, up high

<u>in the Sky! Therefore, win the battle strategically by Flying First Class - on your own territory!</u>

The bible says in (Matthew 7:7 KJV) "Ask, and it shall be given you, seek, and ye shall find; knock, and it shall be opened unto you." Once a vision and plan are followed, it will surely become a reality. Keep moving forward, the reason being, generations are awaiting you to accomplish the vision. It will fulfill your life's purpose and assignment on earth. **Be Happy Visionary! Imagine that.**

ABOUT THE LEADER

Reverand Natalia Monique Lewis

Rev. Monique Lewis is an anointed, gifted, and powerful woman of God that touches so many people through music and the preached Word. She has bridged so many gaps between the young and old everyone can receive the message of Christ through her ministry. She was born on November 21, 1980, and raised in Eden, NC. At the ages of 14-16, she won best young-female pianist at the Waljo People's Choice Awards presented by Bobby Jones, Dorinda Clark

Cole, Nancy Wilson, and Daryl Coley. At age 18, she accepted her calling to preach the Gospel and she started a youth outreach ministry called *Serenity Ambassadors for Christ* reaching youth through music. In 1999, she graduated from Morehead High School located in Eden, NC. She later attended undergraduate studies at Rockingham Community College in which she obtained her Associate in Arts Degree. She continued her education at Oral Roberts University where she completed her Bachelor of Arts Degree in Pastoral Care and minor in psychology. After graduating she still had a passion to gain more knowledge, so she obtained a master's in divinity Degree from Oral Roberts University in 2008. While attending Oral Roberts University, she had the opportunity to play with Wayman Tisdale at Friendship Baptist Church, Keith Childress, and several others. In addition to this, while attending Oral Roberts University she was a part of a music album for Oral Robert's Souls A Fire entitled "Fire" where she released a new arrangement of Blessed Assurance and co-authored/produced a song entitled "Be Still" with coauthor Marchon Hamilton II. After attending seminary, Rev. Lewis also obtained her Clinical Pastoral Education at Duke University Medical Center. In 2010, she was awarded a scholarship by Dr. Patricia Bailey and attended her missionary school called Global Leadership Training Center. Rev. Lewis has been on several mission's trips serving others Soweto, Africa, Montego Bay, Jamaica, and Haiti. In 2014, Rev. Lewis released her first book entitled "The Pursuit of God, Catch me if you Can." Recently she has been a part of co-authoring with a collaboration book Called to Intercede. She also is prayerfully releasing her first album this year entitled "Fully Committed." Her goal is to start a non-profit agency called Youth in Christ to empower, to equip, and to evangelize youth through the Word and

Gospel Music. *Youth in Christ* also is committed to helping reach at-risk youth to prevent drug abuse, violence, human trafficking, and promote Godly character. To help achieve this there are three dimensions of this ministry that impacts youth, which is *Souled Out, Century 21 Bible Institute*, and Natmon Music. Currently, Monique is the Associate Minister and serves as organist at Little Bethlehem Christian Church located in Eden, NC. Her growth over the years shows how she allows the Lord to use her in ministry and how He has enlarged her territory through her obedience to Christ. Every time she shares her gift she receives more from the Lord. She always uses what God gives her to save, heal, and teach in her ministry.

CHAPTER 12

"You Were Born A Leader"

Reverand Natalia Monique Lewis

From the time, you were in your mother's womb you were called to lead. Leadership began initially in Genesis 1:28, when God blessed Adam and Eve and said to them, "Be fruitful and increase in number; fill the earth and subdue it. Rule over the fish in the sea and the birds in the sky and over every living creature that moves on the ground." Adam and Eve were not just called to lead but you were called to lead also and bring change to this world. As a leader, you are called to mark footprints on this earth; This earth or world should know the value of your leadership. The Bible says, in Romans 8:19, "For the earnest expectation of the creature waits for the manifestation of the sons of God." Do you know the earth and creation is waiting on your leadership to eradicate this world? It is waiting on you to become the Son or the daughter of the Most High God. It is in anticipation for what you will become and what mark you will leave on this world.

I believe that what man should fear are only two things. The first being God and the second is not becoming the full value of what you were intended to be as a leader. So many people die not reaching their full potential as a leader and not making a mark on society. It is imperative that we know that we were born to lead and that everyone has leadership qualities. But being a good leader starts first in the mind. Leadership is a state of mind of position. You must know that you are unique and that you were created to do something that no one else can do. You are irreplaceable. There is no one quite like you and that is why no one else can have your fingerprint. Why would God make everyone else a different fingerprint if he did not want you to be different and just be who you are. I was just telling one of my friends the other day that today we have too many clones. Everybody is competing to be the best clone instead of being the best you that you can become.

Can I tell you something that you should know today? Ok here it is. I will say it. YOU ARE ENOUGH! As a leader, you should know that you are enough to succeed. Regardless of your past failures and challenges God says, you are enough. You have it in your DNA to lead. When you think about your DNA, we know it just comes natural and Mother Nature takes over. In the same manner, you were born with leadership DNA that comes natural to you that takes on its own form or shape to cultivate this generation. So, embrace it! You know for years society has been telling us that we do not have what it takes, or that leaders are only built for certain people group, but that is a lie. We are all called to lead!

So where do we start? I am so glad you asked that question. You start first by leading your family, name those children, name those nieces, and nephews. Adam started by naming those animals. We must make sure that our families are named well and have the signature of Christ. We nurture our families and help them to grow and develop into mature leaders. It is a great responsibility that we must lead our families. In the past, we have seen our mothers, fathers, grandmothers, and grandfathers lead with their traditions and instill in us values and mobility. We have seen them become successful and we have held on to the lessons that they have taught us. So, it is our turn to name those animals. It is our turn to name those family members and help them learn their identity in Christ. We are called to lead and help them live out Godly character and reflect the nature of Christ. We are called to help them live out their family name and we are called to help them become the best leaders they can be.

Next, then our second assignment just as Adam was called to do is to subdue the earth. It is called multiplication. We are called to make disciples! Matthew 28:19 says "Go therefore and make disciples of all nations, baptizing them in the name of the Father and of the Son and of the Holy Spirit, [20] teaching them to observe all that I have commanded you; and lo, I am with you always, to the close of the age. This mandate is not just for the elite or ministers this mandate is for every believer. So that means we must lead others to Christ. Wow! You mean I have a charge, yes you do. Well, how do you first lead people to Christ? You first lead people to Christ by displaying the character of God. There are no way people will be reached with the Gospel if you do not live the true meaning of the Gospel. Leaders do not just have a title, but they are given leverage and value by the life they live in Christ. We lead by being the example of Christ. I remember attending a leadership course at Oral Roberts University and I will never forget coming to realization that leadership is not just about doing ministry, but it is about being ministry. Your first calling by God as a leader is not to just do but it is to become ministry. I think when people are taught to always do ministry, they become burnout because they are not being ministry.

There is a distinct difference.

So, in this chapter I want you to get the gist about being called to lead. Let us recap. So, you are first called to lead or born to lead by God. Then in this calling, you are first called to lead your families and then you are called to lead others to Christ while here on the earth. There are so many people who get this order mixed up or confused and they forget about their families in their pursuit to save the world. No, that is not correct. Leadership starts in your individual house and then you minister to others because guess what? You were born to lead for such a time as this.

ABOUT THE LEADER

Tracey Rollie

My name is Tracey Rollie Washington. I am from Chester PA, but I reside in Drexel Hill, Pa. I am a wife, mother, daughter, sister. I have an amazing, blended family who I love. My husband Mike has been a blessing to my life. My first born Xytaha is strong and beautiful. My son Lewis is my prayer warrior and music instructor. My bonus son Seth is my quiet child who is a notable example. My last Seed Linda Marie she is our unexpected baby who is so loving. My parents are Jackie Hudnell and Omar Rollie. My stepfathers are Gary Harris and Kenny Hudnell they have played a Hugh part in my house. I was led to create this business by faith. God let me know it was needed. I face trial and tribulation throughout my life which never stop me. I never understood why so much were coming my way. I created Godstrength Resource and custom Apparels when the pandemic first starts in 2020. I was facing difficulties situation but i noticed while facing things in life. I always had people that would come to me for help which I did not mind because I love helping people. I have helped many people over the years. Godstrength Resource is a company that help the community with Resources and funds. There was a time where I did not know where to find Resources. I had to deal with my situation along. I always was told that leadership was inside of me. I had to go through my own process. This platform is to help community to find and search for resources. It is geared for woman, men, and kids. I have some amazing resources. I try to get involved with leadership at work which I am now a lead caregiver who help the elderly.

CHAPTER 13

What is Leadership?

Tracey Rollie

The action of leading a group of people or an organization: I did not know where to start so I went to talk to my pastor for directions. She helps me out in many ways. I prayed and prayed until God said this is it. Do it afraid and watch the Lord work. There has been time as a business owner that can be very discouraging because you see so many other achievements and you like Lord when is my time. In those seasons is the time to see what you need to improve so that you can be the best business owner you can be.

Being a business owner has shown me stuff about myself to be a better leader. We must take every step that is needed. Our business will take time to take off. Nothing happened overnight. I have taken on the role as a leader at work because they never gave me the position, but I always show up as a lessee which encourages me to show up even better. I will be a formidable leader. I learn to be on time for whatever I do because that is part of being an impressive leader. I learn to prepare so I can be a formidable leader. My family looks up to me as a leader. We must lead by example to our workers when having a business. If we show up right, then the people showing in our company will show up right. When being a leader the way we show up matters.

I had to update my presentation when it came to doing vending events with my products. We must make sure our customers understand when we show up. I am always at my event 20 minute early which Always gets me a great spot. My mom always said it is good to be on time. My goal for my business is to help the community with Resources and funds.

My business is called Godstrength Resource and custom Apparels. My book is called God Strength Devotional which you can find on Amazon. How has it been starting your business? Does it show you think about yourself that you need to change? Sometimes we create things with the wrong mindset, but God will redirect you back to what he plans you to do. I started my business and just took off. When do I say I was so overwhelmed? I would want my first job to come home to my job along with working on my business, going to church and it was too much. I was not spending my time wisely so God sat me down so I could reset my whole life. Want I sit and balance my life. I had more energy and patience and things started to run as they should. We must do things right now not always about getting rich or before someone else, but we must run our business the right way.

Leadership is about leading a company. You must be a great leader. Leadership is a process. You will have to strive as you are growing and learning in your business. I am training my children to do what I do so I can retire by age 50. What has been a challenge as a business owner? Has it made you a greater business owner? What have you learned from being a leader? How was it with starting your business? What have you offered other business owners? Have you done business events so people know who you are? Are you willing to travel with your business? What has been so losses while creating your business.

ABOUT THE LEADER

Shawon Shericka James

Shawon Shericka is a spiritual NAY-Slayer, & native of Brooklyn, NY residing in Maryland.

Visionary of Sisters Overcoming & Winning, LLC (SOW) a community of over 5k warrior sisters, on a mission to edify women through Philanthropy, Kingdom Living, and Evolutionary Leadership. Shawon is a Best-Selling Author, TV Show Host, TV Channel Owner, and Chief Human Resource Officer with Believe in

Your Dreams TV Network, where Dr. Nichole Peters serves as the CEO and Owner. Shawon is a Board Member for the Erin Levitas Foundation for Sexual Assault Awareness. She is also, a Regional Director, on the Executive Team in the Multi-Family Apartment Industry.

Shawon's formal education is accredited to Virginia State University (Psychology), Interboro Institute (Pre-Law), and University of Phoenix (Psychology, Management, & Leadership). **Shawon** has successfully completed professional certifications to undergird her passions and purpose (Disney Leadership Institute, Aimco's Fast Track Program, MMHA Education Coursework, IAP, Dr. Matthew Stevenson's Leader School- just to name a few.

Shawon has accepted her divine assignment to galvanize, nurture, and serve as a midwife to women across national boundaries, as they own and unapologetically encounter a head-on collision with past traumas and promises fulfilled. ***Shawon*** shared stirring excerpts from her life- in a LIVE, one woman shows, April 2021. **Shawon** was Featured in Women of Destiny Top 40 Media Boss Magazine, in August 2021. Shawon has been interviewed by the likes of Les Brown, Kim Jacobs, Pastor Jason Hendrickson, and others.

Shawon has shared her gift and passion of spoken word at several women's events, forums, and panel discussions. ***Shawon*** is an Intentionality Midwife (Coach) who devoutly serves as a Minister of the Gospel, at Renewed Hope Church, Linthicum, Maryland, under the Pastoral Leadership of Bishop Jammie and Pastor Kenise Pendleton. ***Shawon*** has a heart for philanthropy, servitude, and all things overcoming and winning! She is a loving and proud mom two amazing adult children!

The adversary attempted to devour her **YES** to God, but - Jeremiah 1:5, is her portion.

Shawon is committed to adding some weight to her "dash," as she humbly pursues all that God has for her. "My mother named me ***Shawon Shericka*** but, my FATHER calls me ***Appointed***"!

Shawon's website is www.sowinning.org

Facebook & YouTube: Shawon ShaSha Shericka, Intentionally Spoken TV & Sisters Overcoming and Winning (SOW).

Instagram: Intentionally Spoken Tv & Sisters Overcoming and Winning.

TikTok: Shawon ShaSha Shericka.

Email: sistersovercomingandwinning@gmail.com & intentionallyspokenpod@gmail.com

CHAPTER 14

"Don't Forget the Sugar and Eggs"

Pericope for Scripture Reference: Matthew 20:26-28

Shawon Shericka James

Whether you are preparing banana nut muffins, apple muffins, cornbread, or sweet potato muffins- the recipe requires sugar and eggs! Be it granulated, cane, brown, or stevia (healthy option) as a sweetener- sugar is required. You also need, an egg (or two). If anyone begs to differ, do not eat their muffin - LOL, you have been warned! I guarantee, no one will ask for seconds if either ingredient is missing. Without sugar and eggs, the muffin is bland, wasteful, and purposeless. Ultimately, picked over and discarded because no one would be able to stomach it.

Those who are "Called to Lead" must be anchored in the humility, humanity, servitude, and most certainly- love or else, the ministry, business, work environment, and/or your home/family will be bland, wasteful, and without purpose – just like those muffins.

Your authority is not reliant upon your title; there are specific people assigned to your unique anointing. Let us tarry in this space for a moment. When you are "called" God is summonsing your gifts to break ground, break chains, break-through, break norms, take root, and cultivate a series of continuous manifestations of the authority that innately resides in your DNA as member of God's kingdom.

Jeremiah 1:5 is our reminder -before the seed, being you and I, was planted in our mother's womb, God knew us. He established in the earth realm, that we would pastor (lead/shepherd) the masses. This affirms that we are predestined, divinely elected (God approved) and equipped (having the tools needed) to garner the assignment before our lungs were formed.

When God calls you, your only response should be to yes. Honestly, answering the call is easy but, dwelling in the call is a challenge. The people that you are called to lead will come with obstacles and situations. Bottomline, people will be, people– let them be. Your responsibility is to obey the instruction without regard for the detriment of being uncomfortable, persecuted, judged, ridiculed, and profusely met with contention about your ability and/or effectiveness to lead.

Beloved – your calling will COST you!!! It **SHALL** (*definitely*) cost you!!! As you say 'Yes' to God, relationships will dissolve without warning or explanation. Your health, job, finances, business, and home will simultaneously become bottomless and unrecognizable. Everything that you previously considered solid, will become disheveled, in disarray, and discombobulated. There will be nothing you can do to halt or reverse it. You must locate peace, from the peace giver and settle in. This seems bizarre especially after you finally, submitted an unwavering 'YES' -you would think life gets easier. Nope, not at all. Your YES- flipped, everything upside down. Have you ever accidentally left a bag opened or a beverage uncovered while driving, then there is a sudden stop and the contents spills everywhere, making an utter mess? When this happens in the natural, it is a mishap; but spiritually- God allows the mess to bless us. We must divorce everything that blemishes kingdom credibility and character. Leaders must remain steadfast and accountable especially when absent from sacred spaces.

When you are in position to empty your carnal traits, God fills you with more peace, understanding, compassion, servitude, obedience, righteousness, "act right" LOL, and most importantly – LOVE!

Kingdom Leadership is not predicated upon rank or a system, like that of a food chain. A leader who is called, is pre-qualified unlike a credit pre-approval when they still screen for credit worthiness. The favor on your calling grants immediate access, bypassing security checkpoints and authentication procedures to assess your qualifications (anointing). There is no waiting list or paperwork, to prove who you are when God has appointed you. When you are "Called to Lead," every room (at home, workplace, place of worship, supermarket, etc.) your name is mentioned, permits kingdom authority. You must be engaged and married to the labor required of your assignment.

There is an assignment with your name embossed upon. It requires action and work, as the bible declares- otherwise it is dead. The anointing is equipped to fulfill the assignment. Jeremiah 1:5, is a fervent reminder that a divine appointment that was established before your parents met. Before your existence, there was an expectation for your life. Read that again – (**pause**) now, shout – HALLELUJAH AND THANK YOU LORD! The subsequent portion of that pericope of scripture proclaims that you shall be a priest to the masses. The word "shall" infer that you will absolutely be a shepherd over the masses.

Your title only establishes ministry birth order, not qualification. We live in a time of quick fixes and accelerated presence. There is no short cut to what God has ordained; however, there are privileges for those who are called. Establish your response on a solid foundation. A wise leader creates a foundation built on the rock, of salvation- being Christ! (Psalm 18:2). Every "building" or established household, business, worship edifice and/or a person must be rooted in Christ. Christ is all things love (sugar) and servitude (eggs); make these your foundational pillars. Love is law, do all things in love (2 Corinthians 16:14). A Called Leader -convicts in love, corrects in love and creates covenant in love.

Leaders must have the capacity to push pass people issues, internal insecurities, validation, materialistic possessions, and the pit of hell. Remain postured, declaring "Lord, now I trust me – so you can trust me with more

Remain keenly aware to discern the adversary's assignment to devour God's assignment. It is dangerous, to trust our natural eye, over our spiritual eye; especially, when our destiny is blood soaked in prosperity! The advancement of the body of Christ by way of witnessing and boasting of the sovereign Father we love and serve- adds weight to our lives and life to the call.

When you are "Called to Lead" the assignment is not about you, your story is a template for others to recognize that deliverance, salvation, and healing for their situation is available through Christ.

Leaders do the work. Followers, see the need then, wait for others to initiate the work. If you desire the recognition and title, then work for it with purpose and passion. You are "Called to Lead" the people out of Egypt, be encouraged for the one who endures, earns the spoils. Lead by example and in excellence. Please be sure to add the love and servitude (aka eggs and sugar) to make your Leadership and Calling palatable as you stand in and on a firm YES, to Lead! Blessings, Beloved!

Made in the USA
Middletown, DE
09 April 2023